# TWILIGHT

## JAY GRIFFITHS

HEDGESPOKEN PRESS
2018

TWILIGHT is part of the *Seven Doors in an Unyielding Stone* series.

The titles in the series are:

See WWW.HEDGESPOKENPRESS.COM/SEVEN-DOORS
for more about the series.

# TWILIGHT

IT IS TWILIGHT and at the waking edge of night, a crescent otter breaks the surface of the water, looping up from its dive, in its mouth a crescent fish shines silver, a little late moon.

Night chases day like one otter cub chasing another. *Otter ludens*, they are creatures of play, on the margins of day, and they fathom both air and water, influent in the element that becomes them. Every otter is a play on words, a one-word pun, for the word 'otter' is related to the word 'water.'

My kitten is called Otter. It is apt. He is ludic from nose to paws. He often sleeps like an otter at rest, on his back with his paws neatly meeting over his tummy. He has diurnal spurts of joyful playfulness, one at dawn and the other at dusk when he mews imperiously at me until I join him in playing with a toy mouse, and then he hurls himself in curly crazy circles around anything. He is also black and white, sporting the livery of twilight.

Meanwhile at dusk 'the sky is darkening,' wrote a Neapolitan of the seventeenth century, 'darkening to the colour of a wolf's snout.' Among the trees, a pine marten runs a quicksilver streak, mercury in motion. It freezes even faster than it flows and is gone.

I hear a badger, grunting, shoving stones aside: he means business. Then I see him, touched by two light, day-streaked and night-stroked, a piano keyboard playing a twilight sonata in a minor key for the maligned creatures of twilight, the badgers themselves, the wolf, the hare and the bat – flittermouse in flights of arpeggios to catch moths. And owls.

From nowhere – and in utter silence – a barn owl slips between the trees, as if there is barely a feather between this world and the other. Only one sense registers it, not hearing or scent or touch, only sight. The eye struggles to see, tries harder than it does in the easy light of day. This is the difficult, bewildering light, where a tree stump with its black fingers of roots looks like a badger, and the eye must tug objects back into their proper outlines as the wind ruffles leaves into faces. This is the tricky hour – when the eye plays tricks on you, foxing you with a deer shadow. 'In the night, every cat is a leopard,' as the Italian proverb says. Sight, ruler of the senses during daytime, and untrickable at noon, is now, at dusk, losing power to the insurrection of the other senses.

★

At twilight, I find myself breathing in deeply, as if unconsciously I lean towards scent, drawn like a moth towards the fragrance of some flowers and plants, so strong at dusk, including evening primrose, night-scented stock, jasmine, angel's trumpet, wisteria and honeysuckle. But I find myself smelling things at dusk as if they had simply more to say at that hour. Pub smells. Woodsmoke. Food. The smell of leaves on a wet pavement. I am intrigued by the very air, asking more questions of it. I want to know things 'in the air' as if I too am a bit more of my animal self, and my sense of smell is coming into its own.

Reliance on hearing increases. The body stills itself to feel more, quiets itself to hear more. The word 'listen' is an anagram of 'silent.' In the willing silence the tentative senses are attentive. If there is a dawn chorus, I would suggest there is also a dusk chorus, a westward flow of quiet, a whisperous Hesperus rolling across all the world, slowly, continuously, punctuated by a hare drumming, a coyote howl, or owl hoot at owl-leet, owl-light, which is one term for twilight. Other terms include 'crow-time,' as crows roosted and 'cock-shut' as well as the gloaming or the 'shutting-in,' the time to bring the animals in and bolt the doors. The only word for twilight which I hate is 'crepuscular,' an exoskeletal word, one of the very few words in the English language which is (to my ears) not onomatopoeic.

Night seems to come up from the earth, from the chthonic, if you are out in it. The trees seem to grip the earth with their knuckles now, fingering the black soil. Darkness doesn't fall, it rises from the roots. From indoors, looking out, it does fall, perhaps, in a cadence of sun fall and the autumn, the fall season, is when twilight is most meaningful. Accidents – a nasty fall – happen more often at this hour. Luck, though, too, is associated with twilight – the moment of chance and hazard, how fate befalls, how 'it fell out,' they say in fairy tales. The mischief hour. Because twilight resists duality, it doesn't say lucky or unlucky, it says both chance and mischance, in the hour which is neither night nor day as time swings on its hinges; is night half open or day half closed?

The sky holds a little last handful of light cupped in its west left hand. It is a west-side story. Twilight is the between-light, after sunset and before night when the sun's light is still present in the sky even after the sun is gone. Twilight is an enigmatic reflection, that other word for thinking. Something is in the air, electric and inter-intelligent, in this hour of ambiguity, of paradox, opaquely suggestive. As the reflection of psyche and light are both elliptical, certainty is bewildered, it is a moment when mind is half open to night and star-guided. Only one hour in twelve is a twilight hour, dusk or dawn, and twilight is the trickster in the pack of hours, as Hermes is the trickster of the twelve Olympian gods, on the edge of divinity, the least of them, in the pantheon of Proper Gods.

Something shifts its weight from one foot to the other. Trickster is abroad. Duels are fought. Messengers are heard – or shot. Poems are hunted. Traps are set.

It is the uneasy hour, when predator may become prey, and prey may become predator, because everything which rises must also fall, and everything forced to fall will rise in fury. By twilight, preparations were made for smuggling and owling – the illegal export of wool. 'The landlord robs us all day: we'll rob him all night,' is the nocturnal vow of poachers – predators of animals, prey of gamekeepers. Normal laws of daylight did not – could not – apply. In a famous Welsh tradition if, between twilight and dawn, someone could build a turf cottage on waste or common land, it was theirs forever.

Teenagers belong in twilight; their body clock urging them out, to the 'nocturnal, beastly roaming about,' according to an observer in Paris, 1651. All over Europe, history records how twilight was the hour of 'Lewde youthes,' as reported in Coventry in 1605, running amok in riots and obscenity, German youths yodelling, Danish youths chasing the dark, hell for leather, with horns, bells and trumpets.

The social clock changes. The alteration at dawn from asleep to awake is, if we sleepers allow ourselves, a misty hour, slow and dreamily self-estranged, where the psyche can feel as easily lost as a walker in fog. It is an enormous shift but mostly private. On the streets at dusk, though, the publicly-lived life is transformed from the sensible sober world of daytime work to the happy-hour glee of release, the lid-off bubbling over, people spilling out of bars, beer spilling out of glasses, conversation spilling out of mouths. Day has ended but night has not yet begun. There is a human instinct to gather; we are starlings now in a human murmuration. I feel tugged by something ancient within me, to meet people, to stroll. The longing for a *passeggiata* seems to me to be a universal human yearning, to see and be seen at evening. At dusk, society steps away from the day's curt command to obey Captain Clock. Time itself is on the loose. Hours are as easily and sweetly lost at dusk as they could be at dawn.

Twilight upsets the day, subverting its settled order. The establishment Middle C of daytime rises to an F sharp at dusk, the eerie augmented fourth, the tense, alluring, weird interval, called, famously, the Devil's Interval, used in the opening of West Side Story, and also in Wagner's 'Twilight of the Gods.' It is a loop-hole, a loup-hole, a hole for the wolf (*loup* in French) to pass through. If it is played after Middle C, this is the one of all the twelve notes on a piano keyboard which makes the hairs stand up on the back of your neck. This interval was suppressed by the church of the Middle Ages for creating a space that let the devil in. But this gap, this interval, is necessary to let the trickster in.

At twilight you must mind the gap, the interval, the rift, the opening. Twilight may trouble the day or console it, may pacify or perturb, may treat you or trick you. Trickster is god of the twilight. Trickster is god of the periphery, and for humans our peripheral vision is actually better now than by daylight: this is literally and metaphorically true.

The youngest of Hinduism's gods, the trickster in the Hindu pantheon, is the child Krishna. His skin is the blue of the sky at dusk, and he goes thieving at twilight and dawn, stealing milk and butter, upsetting the householders: a mischievous, naughty, mercurial divinity.

The Trickster of the Greeks was Hermes, called Mercury by the Romans. He was god of border-crossing, god of the waysides, the roads between towns, of no man's land, as twilight is no man's hour. Margin-dweller and double-dealer, an unpredictable god, he promises neither border control nor safe passage. The security guards are asleep and otters have swum into their dreams. Passport control are drunk in charge of a pack of cards, and the joker is playing them. Customs officers have emigrated, twilighting as impressionist painters.

Trickster is reliably unreliable, the riddler, the fiddler, he'll fiddle you: he plays Paganini when Jupiter plays Purcell. Trickster is the riff, he plays you extemporized brilliance in the cadenza, then throws a wolf note to trip you up. He deals in luck, good and bad, but never pays his debts or gives you your due. Trickster will swipe your wages, then give you a windfall. Trickster will light the lantern to let you find your way and then, in a gust of wind, will snuff it out. Trickster is the will o' the wisp, played by Puck, the night flitter and by Robin Goodfellow leading the wanderer astray at night through bogs and forests. Trickster is a joker, least of the gods, and his appearance is only possible within a pantheon of gods. So Mercury among the Olympians, edgy, resisting duality, is neither god or devil, which is why the trickster disappears in monotheism, because the monogod unfairly libels the Trickster, calling him devilish and expelling him into the pitch black night, tarred and crow-feathered.

The raven represents Mercury, but the English language refers, unkindly, to 'an unkindness of ravens' and to a 'murder of crows' as our society murders the creatures of the twilight, who all have something of Mercury about them, pine-marten quicksilver in the woods, and the mercurial 'hare-brained' hare.

Trickster is as playful as an otter but, I've known fishermen say, otters 'steal' their fish. Prometheus and Loki, tricksters both, steal fire. Raven steals fire too, and food – he is ravenous – and sun, stars and moon. Trickster is a thief, the wrong-footing, fly-by-night, tall-tale-teller, latch-lifter, fence-breaker, lock-picker, light-footed, with feathers at his ankles, light-fingered, at twilight Loki is abroad, look to your picked-pocket, my friend, it happens in the interval, the tenner is now a plucked note, the *pizzicato* fingers in the *glissando* of your smooth pocket.

If Trickster is one part of the body, it is the funny-bone. But Trickster is never only one thing: he is the ankle, wrist, hip, knuckle – all the joints of the body as he is god of the joints (the junctions) of the day at twilights. 'Articulus' is a joint in the body and a joint, a turning point, in the year – as the All

Souls Night, May Day, solstices and equinoxes are the ankles, wrists and elbows in articulating the body of the year. It is all an articulate pun. Trickster articulates – Hermes is the messenger and Mercury is god of writers. And all these words link, of course, to art and to the artist, trickster in the pantheon of Proper Jobs.

Jacob is the extraordinary trickster of the Old Testament: the name Jacob means trickster, deceiver, heel-grabber – and, yes, Trickster can cheat and lie – he's a bit of a heel. When he has been wrestling with the Angel all night, at the twilight of dawn, the junction point, the joint of night, the angel admits he cannot defeat Jacob, so touches the hollow of his hip, he goes for the joint. In blessing, the Angel says 'now you will be called Israel because you have contended with god and won.'

Names and their meanings. Words and the roots of words. Signs and the interpretation of signs: all these are the domain of the Trickster, so Hermes, god of signposts, is the messenger and scribe of the gods. Hermes, as the divinity of speech, writing and eloquence, gives his name to hermeneutics, the art of interpretation. Part of his paradox is that his own signs are hard to read; he made himself shoes of branches to hide his footsteps; his messages may be hidden but are treasured when found. Hermes means 'he of the stone-heap' – the cairns of rocks by which a hidden path is revealed, the cairns which protect the traveller from being lost. He is god of what is hidden, or missing.

In terms of metallurgy, hidden gold is found by Mercury, for as mercury only adheres to precious metals, so mercury leads the way to mined gold. In myth, it is Hermes who fetches Persephone from the underworld, so the golden harvests can once more fill the cornfields. The spirit of Hermes travels between ordinary daylight and the deep subconscious of dream, instinct, metaphor, and poetry, coming back with the mind gold. He goes by twilight, the hidden hour, the cairn hour, when the cairn is most important to travellers, the hour of lost time.

★

Every day at twilight, I lose my way. My path through the day usually seems clear. I can walk fine. Until dusk. Then I sink. I stumble. I feel changed. I can work hard in the day, whether it is writing or housework or generally fixing things. Come dusk, though, something happens. I flag. But this is not exactly tiredness or hunger. I feel that I have lost my path. I need to look around, check where I am and what is happening. I am not anxious, but alert in a very different way to that of my daytime self. I am stilled inside, but sensitive to the world. I may be both predator and prey. I feel a quivering kind of electricity. But the strongest feeling is that of being temporarily lost.

I need to look for my bearings. I want a cairn, some sign of significance, quick, feathered, fleet, lively. I want to catch the news which most enjoys the dawn and dusk, for Mercury is god of the best of the media, the Naughtie presenters of dawn and Mair mischief-makers at dusk. Mercury, of course, was once a common name for newspapers. Or I want a fire, stolen by the trickster for the twilight hours, and the fire's presence will create a certainty of both place and time. I want to know the social news, or get a message or hear a story; something of Hermes.

For some, twilight is the hour of whispered vespers. For others the hour of hesitant tryst, hesperous and suggestive. For others yet, the hour of the quiet swindle, the twilight robbery of the conman. It is the hour of the voice whether news-telling, at prayer, at question, at deception, at promise, the hour of the voice at story – not any particular story, but the story of story, to see things otherwise, neither black nor white but open to interpretation. People gathered, traditionally, at twilight, for knitting or spinning evenings, and told stories, spinning tales, twilight inside twilight, the ever curious mind trying to see in the dark: what happened next?

By twilight, the mind may want to offer the silence into which other voices may speak. Or the oceanic feeling into which a dream can swim. The uncurtaining, the rift, the torn veil, the mind open to the presence of what is usually ignored.

At twilight, the innerness of things is outered. Twilight has an inside. You can climb into its cocoon, curl up there, hear a tale take you anywhere, as vastness becomes intimate and the intimate vast. In this interior hour, the daytime's team-spirit solidarity melts into the thinner air; it is the hour of the solitaries, now, alone, together, an encounter of different kinds of solitudes. I have spent hours at twilight, solitary, waiting for the other solitaries: badger, hare, pine-marten, owl. And there, though, I find the paradox of solitudes: alone and never alone, I am part of the twitching, whiskered, sniffing, alert, listening world.

Twilight is a state of mind. Thought flits silent between trees, a feather for your thoughts? I am owling the night.

Language too easily equates light with knowledge – it came to light that; she lit on an idea; in the logic of Enlightenment. Logos sets its fixed ratios with the rational sun, but in its setting, Mythos stirs and rises, cannier than we can know at noon. Twilight, twolight, reminds us every day that the psyche is a twice-dweller, fluent in other languages intuited by night. 'Evening words are not like to morning,' as the traditional English proverb says. When day shuts up its shout, twilight mind asks dusk to usher in its utterances.

We say 'it dawns on me' but not 'it dusks on me.' Yet that way of knowing is a deft vision as the mind, free of daylight jesses, is ownerless as an owl and deeper than it appears on the surface. I have sunk my fingers to the second knuckle deep down in the feathers of the tawny owl before I have touched its tiny body. Minerva is the goddess of wisdom and, they said, 'The owl of Minerva comes at dusk.'

The mind in its own twilight wonders, questions, interprets, prays and wishes. Every modality is twilit – maybe-minded, it might be, could be, would be, it longs to reach out, stretch this elastic hour for its mystery and meaning. For now there is moonrise in the mind and the poet is listening, thinking the world by twolight, the actual and metaphoric. There are no horizons to the mind, now, no limit to its insight.

The mind leans to twilight, to see further than what appears, searching for what it means. The mind is remembering its roots.

Tangled, knotty, subterranean, in the Indo-European root *men*. Its derivatives include the English 'mind' and 'remember.' In Old Norse *muninn* means 'memory' or 'mind,' and is the name of one of Wotan's ravens sent out at dawn, to gather information and to return at twilight with the news. Its companion raven is Huginn, from the Old Norse word for 'thought.' There is wisdom that comes by twilight, the story says.

★

But the shouty and powerful gods of modernity threaten the creatures of twilight, hating the wild minds of teenagers, loathing the raven and crow and planning to exterminate the badgers with a cruelty only matched by its stupidity. Ours is an age of gods engineering our own twilight, banging the seasons together and buckling the year until harvests so willing, Demeter, Ceres, so serially willing cancel their yields, the cornfields are not golden but ashen, and Hermes can no longer recover Persephone.

The twilight of the gods was brought about when the laws of the gods were broken, the World Ash Tree cut down. These are the bone stories, told in the marrow, created from a species-unease at what we feared we could do, a society playing for real its own Endgame, where instead of 'All that rising corn! And there! Look! The sails of the herring fleet!' all we can see is ashes. 'What dreams!' writes Beckett, 'Those forests.'

Dreams, says George Steiner, 'can be the last refuge of freedom and the hearth of resistance.' In ancient times, dreams were not considered to be personal but were messages from the gods, the dreamer the messenger. Every dreamer is Hermes by night.

★

And this was my dream. It was a dream to break my heart, to crack my mind like a twisted rubik cube. It was lightning in the noon of night; it split my sleep apart like an axe splits a log. A hot sleep, reeking midnight and I woke on the stroke of twelve, my head aching, on a night when all that's left is the truth.

It was a dream of the fury of the beasts, a living lightning shaking the world to speech until in its ferocity it shrieks a dream from the subsoil. Everything is breakable. Everything wounded beyond forgiveness.

With a collective refusal to think by twilight, modernity has wrenched a world out of true and something – a kind of cosmic patience – has snapped. Crow has got the searchlights out, coldly turning human movement to carrion. Mole is hammering nails through the gamekeeper's wrists and knees, hanging him upside down on a gibbet as a warning to others. Bat scribbles slogans on his face. There was a loop-hole in my night and the wolf leapt in, cracking a mobile phone in her knucklebones, radio-tracking a herd of men and women to coordinate our fleeings. Hare has raced the pilots to the planes and won, he has picked up the knack of the opposable digit and is flying drones against us. Hare-brained no longer, he pilots the sun into cornfields to strafe them with fire. The quicksilver pine marten is laying exquisite traps of mercury to poison us with our own trick. Badger, perhaps angrier than any, has taken the spade from every garden shed and sharpened the edge to silver and is digging upwards, slicing up into our ankles like you'd strike at a hated rootwad of brambles and as he does he strikes sparks off the flints in my ankle bones, as I sleep.

We kill the badger and libel the wolf, speak evil of the owl-leet and turn the flittermouse to comics. We hate them, the twilight ones, and now their loathing comes back at us. Bruised by my dream and my ankles screaming, I say: 'But I'm on your side, I am part of the Resistance, I've been on your side all my life. I am a Partisan.' 'Then this is a message,' came the terse, furious reply.

I am jolted awake by an electricity of mind, I am cattle prodded, flung, still dreaming, into a kind of wakefulness, a twilight state of mind. And I lay unable to sleep, unable to wake, dreamwrecked till three.

★

And Otter? What of him? He is there in the potent penumbra. Now waking, now sleeping, playing the edges, riffing on the shores, *Otter ludens*, like my mind half on the dry land of being surely awake, and half in waters of sleep. My Otter, meanwhile, kitten of the half and half, of dawn and dusk, is now lying on his back, wrapped in the kelp of deep sleep and dreaming our better dreams.

HEDGESPOKEN PRESS *publishes works of beauty, power and old magic in the form of the printed word and image.*

*To keep up with what we do, please subscribe to our newsletter at:*
WWW.HEDGESPOKENPRESS.COM